THE WILL OF GOD:
Bringing My Children Home

To support your healing journey, these too are
offered by
Robert Weltman PhD

Website
Christian Laity Foundation
www.christianlaityfoundation.org

Radio
Spiritual Healing Radio
Broadcasting on WTBQ out of New York
www.wtbq.com

YouTube
Healing Aspirations
Available via Healing Aspirations Channel
www.youtube.com/christianlaityfound

Books (Coming Soon)
The Footladder of Notes Divine – Yearly Devotionals
used daily to support one's healing journey
Come as You Are: The Love of God
Mary: Mother God
The Footladder of Notes Divine

God speaks to the Reader:

"This book speaks of Me and for Me.
I choose to speak for it.
It provides you with Me in the sense and scope
of My healing power and salvific mission.
I cherish its contents.
I am your God of unconditional love."

The Son can do nothing of Himself
but what He sees the Father do;
for whatever He does,
the Son also does in like manner.

(John 5:19 – The New King James Version)

There is but one truth.
Ye are gods and ye are loved.

(The Footladder of Notes Divine, 7/11/2012)

Lost in time
do we sanctify evil
and bless curses.

(The Footladder of Notes Divine, 4/3/2013)

THE WILL OF GOD:
Bringing My Children Home

Robert Weltman PhD

Other Robert Weltman PhD books can be purchased through our website at www.christianlaityfoundation. org or through your local bookstore, Amazon, Baker & Taylor, Ingram and Barnes & Noble. All proceeds go to Christian Laity Foundation.

EDITOR: LYNNE MATOUS

PUBLISHER: CHRISTIAN LAITY FOUNDATION PUBLISHING; MIDDLETOWN, NEW YORK 10940

COVER & INTERIOR DESIGN: KIM TARONJI & NIKI JONES AGENCY INC.

LIBRARY OF CONGRESS CONTROL NUMBER: 2013957262

ISBN: 978-0-9890686-0-4

FIRST EDITION

Dedication

To the service of our precious, loving God and Savior.

Thank you God for your role in creating this book and providing its title and recommendations of its content to enhance its meaningfulness to those of your children for whom You intend it.

Table of Contents

Acknowledgements

I thank the God of absolute unconditional love guiding us in the making of this book. You are the single source of any and all goodness found within it. We affirm your healing presence for the followers whom you've made ready to receive it.

I credit Kim and Enzo Taronji as the driving force insisting that this book be written and also for their influence and support with the production of the book in its entirety. I thank Lynne Matous for the gentle, necessary final editing that strengthened the clarity of the material within. I recognize Reverend William Johnston, Sandy Moneymaker, Father John Warfel, Reverend Dr. Jon Mundy, Danielle Taronji and Noelle Pollet for their contribution in reviewing the manuscript and supporting its teaching curriculum. I thank Jesse Holt for the typing and initial editing of the manuscript and for all her abiding support. I am grateful for my son David Weltman for his computer support, keeping me connected to the project. I am also indebted to the WTBQ staff Frank Truatt, Rich Ball, and Souzie Miller for their backing of the project and maintenance with our radio show, Spiritual Healing Radio. A special thanks to Olga Zernhelt who has supported this movement since its inception and who was integral in establishing associations with our marketing agency. And lastly, much gratitude to Niki Jones, Peter Bertino, Stephanie Brynes, Kate Palermo and Danielle Correia for the creative input, public relations, project management and marketing of this holy project.

Preface

You've got a healing coming and you most certainly will get it! You've reached the perfect time in your life, ready and willing, led by God to find this book on healing. It's the same place that Dr. Bob was at, putting aside the standard professional beliefs about healing, to make room for God to deliver the spiritual approach to full well-being.

"The Will of God: Bringing My Children Home" demonstrates the path on how and why you'll get back home. You've reached the unique place in your life where you reflect upon your personal issues that cause you uneasiness. You want answers. Who am I? What am I doing in this world? Am I lovable? How did I get here in the first place? Do I die? Is there an afterlife? Is there a God? Why am I depressed or anxious? Why do I drink or do drugs? Are there answers? Is peace possible?

You're seeking solutions to overcome the human mind. Can it be overcome? A resounding YES! Peace and self-confidence await us. In this book, Dr. Bob shares with us the answers, how they come to us and from Whom. Do you know what that will do for you?

Since your spirit mind is one with God's mind, you can handle any moment, any circumstance, and any relationship in the same way, the same manner as God would and achieve the same results as would God. Everything works out to your best interest and to the best interest of those around you. Would you like that perfection available to you while in this world?

God blessed this book by personally providing its

title, then addressing the quality of the book's content by stating to you, the reader, "Feast upon the love of God" and finally by proclaiming its value in your ultimate healing and salvation with the statement, "This book has won God's seal of approval." We can't wait for you to experience God's involvement in and delivery of your ultimate healing; *the will of God is bringing all of His children home!*

How God Gets You Home

It's no accident that you're reading this book. You've gotten to the wonderful point in your life that you're looking at your personal issues that cause you uneasiness. You want answers.

Who am I? What am I doing in this world? How can I consistently feel good about myself? How can I feel self-confident in my circumstances and my relationships? How can I end moments of being shaken up by my feelings of self-doubt? Withstand other's criticism?

Am I lovable? Is there anyone out there who cares about me?

What is this world about? Why am I here? How did I get here in the first place?

Do I die? Does the "me" have an end? Is there an afterlife?

Is there a personal God? What does God feel about me?

Will I ever overcome my anxieties and fears? How can I deal with my feelings of bone-deep loneliness and fear of rejection? Are there solutions to my depressed feelings? Drinking problems? Substance abuse? Self-punishment? Anger at others?

Is there a place of peace that I can bask in? Are there answers? Hello anyone, can you help? What do I do with my guilt about what I've done in the past? Some pretty cruddy things. Or how I degrade myself, or let others degrade me? Can I even get the courage to share these things? To tell anybody? To overcome my shame about what I feel I am?

You're seeking answers to overcome *the human*

mind. Can it be overcome? A resounding *YES!* Our human mind can be overcome. Peace and self-confidence await us. I share with you the answers that I have received thus far in my own life and applied to my life, how they come and from Whom.

Ten years of personal analysis, a doctoral degree program in Psychology, my work in psychiatric hospitals, on college campuses, in private practice, as the head of the psychology program in a forensic psychiatric center for the criminally insane, in drug rehabilitation work, in our local jail, with the homeless, invariably focused on the standard beliefs of those times in order to overcome problems. One must CORRECT THE HUMAN MIND, ITS BELIEFS AND EMOTIONAL STATES. I used techniques ranging from rationalizing how improper the human mind's thoughts were; looking at past experiences as the cause of present problems; role playing catharsis of one's feelings as the healing basis; all these the standard tools of the practice of psychotherapy. I don't deny that it was helpful to me and to others with whom I worked, but my understanding grew to the point where I knew the human mind WAS NOT CHANGEABLE.

The solution was different. Instead of changing the human mind, one had to abandon it in order to recover our divine mind, which sat inside us and could surface if we knew the process for uncovering and activating it.

If we could not recover our divine mind, *created to be in oneness with God, and always absolutely untroubled, joyous, and content,* then we were stuck with our human mind. Day after day, no matter what ways we addressed it; the human mind repeated its litany of inadequate self-esteem, loneliness, depression, defensiveness, fears of others' opinions of us and finally death and nothingness. The end of us.

I am so joyful at being granted the understanding by God about what true healing comes down to and how to achieve it. It has been the basis of my latter years of helping others to recover their *divine mind*, its untroubled and peaceful content, both while in this world and in the world to come when we return to the spirit dimension.

Read on to grasp the foundation for your and all peoples' healing, for ultimately the reason behind our troubled state is a simple one, and the solution is simple as well. Hopefully this book will reveal the framework of healing to you and provide you with new and helpful insights into your issues, which are everybody's issues, not just yours alone.

Ultimately, the reasoning that drives you is simple. If you believe that the real you is mortal, you are going to do everything you possibly can to make sure that you'll survive in this world, no matter what you've got to do in order to stay alive. After all, you'll believe that your life is limited to a certain period of time, and then when that time runs out you're dead.

Now that's frightening! For you'll think the world goes on for another gazillion years and you never exist again. You're gone. No more you. No more thinking. No more feeling. Non-existence. Dead. Those conclusions drive the person who thinks that the human life is the only life into frantic desperation.

But death is real. Doesn't everybody die?

Sure it seems real, if you believe that you have but one self and it's a human one, and lives in the world of time, space and embodiment. But, thank God, there is another self that we all have. It's a spirit self, it lives forever, and has an entirely different nature then this seemingly real human self. I know that in your life you have probably been exposed to the teachings of at least one or a few religious philosophies, and yet, here you are, still searching and living this desperate life focused on the world that surrounds you. Your journey needs to take you to the next step in which you might not as yet believe... you must know that there is a spiritual you that will go on!

How did I find it out?

God showed me my spirit self; just like Jesus took three of His disciples up a mountain and turned into a brilliant white light before them, showing another dimension to them that wasn't human. Then to top it off, Elijah and Moses, who the disciples knew had been dead long, long ago, appeared in front of them, showing them their spirit self-existence.

Many of our religious traditions support the existence of the spirit dimension. For instance, in Judaism, the prophets Isaiah, Jeremiah and Ezekiel are brought out of this world into the presence of God. Moses' paranormal experience of gazing at the burning bush, which is not being consumed by the fire, prepares him to experience God's presence, and still later on, to witness God walking before him.

So early on in my healing path, God took me out of my body into the spirit dimension so there should be no doubt of its existence. I had to see this in order to begin to move away from my human self. I know that this might sound frightening and to some extent "mystical"; but if you keep reading, I can show you that it is a natural and welcome experience. History is full of people that have talked to God. And you probably have conversations (even if you make them one way) regularly with Him in your prayers.

This spiritual state is achievable by all. After all, you have a soul, too, and it is patiently waiting for you to re-discover it. And when you are in this spirit mind, you will find yourself in the presence of God too! So, the purpose of this book is to help take YOU on a path that will allow God to show you the same.

Interestingly, just seeing it doesn't make you believe that immortality exists for you. The disciples remained frightened until they FELT IT INSIDE THEMSELVES ON PENTECOST. It would take thirteen years for me before I, like the disciples, was shown and experienced my immortal self. You'll be prepared for that realization in a slow, gentle fashion, just as I and the disciples were.

So what is my spirit self like?

I can tell it to you, but my telling you doesn't mean that you'll be able to accept the truth of it; not until you've experienced it yourself. As "doubting Thomas" said when the disciples tried to convince him that Jesus had returned from the dead and stood before them; -"I have to see it to believe it." Thomas was right. YOU MUST HAVE A PERSONAL EXPERIENCE OF THE REALITY OF THE SOUL AS YOU. We can support your hope for it, but the clincher is that you are shown the reality of the existence of your divine soul by God, when God gets you ready for it.

My soul had none of the fear producing characteristics that I experience about myself from my human mind and consciousness. It's absolutely at peace. Nothing bothers it. It has no worries, no self-doubts, and no unsuredness. In some of the experiences God appears. Wouldn't you think that I'd panic? After all, I'm no sweetheart in my human state. There is no way my human consciousness can accept unconditional love of myself or others. I'm judgmental, just as much as you, both of myself and others. I'm chronically lonely, insecure, worried about my worthiness, what other people think of me, and unsure about the future.

All the human "stuff" was gone. My soul mind or my spirit mind had taken over. I was complete. I was loved by God. I belonged in the spirit world, the kingdom, heaven.

So what is this book all about? Well, let's be clear on one thing. When you get to heaven, you will be happy and fear free FOREVER!!! What this book is intended to do is to help bring the experience of the peace and joy of that spiritual eternal life to your mind's awareness while you still remain in this world.

Do you know what that will do for you? Since your spirit mind is one with God's mind, you can handle any moment, any circumstance, any relationship in THE SAME WAY, THE SAME MANNER AS GOD WOULD AND ACHIEVE THE SAME RESULTS HE WOULD. EVERY THING WORKS OUT TO YOUR BEST INTEREST AND TO THE BEST INTEREST OF THOSE WITH WHOM YOU MIGHT BE INVOLVED. Would you like that perfection present for yourself while in this world? Yes? Well, hello heaven, goodbye world. God's will is bringing me home!

What You Are Going To Discover

From what we've laid out so far, let's look at the good news that is ahead for you.

First, God intends to bring your soul back home to heaven. Nothing can thwart God's intention. Your soul's mind is at peace there only. Nowhere else.

Second, God is going to show you that your true identity is an eternal spirit being, which is how you were created in the first place. This <u>must</u> be shown to you. This will counter your belief that your one and only identity is a body that is born, lives for a while and then dies.

Third, God will reveal to you that your soul has retained its identity and awareness of itself as a loving being in the eyes of God, and accepts God's opinion of itself as the right and valid one.

Fourth, you are shown that your bodily being and the fearful, lonely world in which it lives have nothing whatsoever to do with God's creating it. God created you in the likeness and the image of Himself. He makes no mistakes! Therefore, you remain that; -an eternal spirit whose home is in heaven and who is dearly loved by God, perfect in all ways. YOU WILL KNOW THIS. IT WON'T BE A MATTER OF FAITH OR HOPE OR WISH. YOU MUST KNOW THE TRUTH OF IT AND GOD WILL PROVIDE THAT TO YOU. Then you will understand Jesus' statements in the Gospels that "It is the spirit that gives life, the flesh has nothing to offer (John 6:63), and "Is it not written in your Law: I said you are gods (John 10:34)". We are spirit beings as created by God and the world of the flesh is nothing; not created by God.

Fifth, no matter what has happened in this world of time, space and bodies, God's process of returning you is based on His creation of you and the recovery of that awareness. Your return of <u>you</u> to your true eternal self and life in the treasured kingdom of heaven is assured. The only matter left to you is your desire to return, which God awaits before your planned return is activated, and its perfect timing decided upon by a God who gently and reassuringly guides you through.

Sixth, once you permit God to activate that process of return, your job is done; and your entire life is now in God's hands for Him to run. God will enable you to abandon your belief in the realness of this world, show you the preciousness of the spirit being that you are and the loving state within which it exists. This enables you to see the desirability of returning to heaven and permit God to enable that return. You will joyously look forward to saying hello to heaven and goodbye to this world with no regrets whatsoever.

Does this mean that once you permit God to activate your return that you drop dead on the spot and leave this world? Absolutely not! Look at the stories of Israel's three major prophets; Isaiah, Ezekiel and Jeremiah. All three offer themselves to serve God, witness to the presence of God and the spirit world, but return again to the human world after that. Why? Because those of us who are shown the treasures of the spirit state, who experience the presence of the loving God, continue to teach in the human world from those revelations, assisting others in their salvation process as well. It is only after our job is completed in helping others to whom we disciple for God, that we are ready to leave this no longer valued world for the one and only true Creation and its ultimate and complete joys.

I use myself as an example as well. Through God's grace, I have seen the treasure of the spirit dimension, and gladly affirm the total lack of worth in this world, yet I have remained to pass this knowledge on to others. But once this is accomplished, there is nothing that holds me in this world. And God will pick an appropriate moment when I easily pass over to my blessed home.

Resolving Uneasiness About God's Attitude Toward You

If you've gotten this far, it would seem you're comfortable with what you've read. And from here on I'm going to share with you the methodology I use in prayer and meditation. It has been working for me, and others with whom I share it. In groups which I facilitate, we have seen God moving the members to deepening awareness of their inner spirit being and the blessed peace and assurance that is delivered to them by which to deal with their issues and life circumstances while they remain in this world.

So, let's begin. I have to discuss one issue with you that needs resolution before going into the prayer and meditation practices. Since prayer and meditation means communication with God, we need to look at your beliefs about how God feels about you. This is crucial. You can't go to God until you feel comfortable and safe. Why? Because the essence of the prayer life that we will be talking about requires a surrender to God's intentions for you.

So, now the question- "Do you feel safe handing yourself over to God for whatever God's will is for you?" Would you say "Yes, absolutely." No worries about God's opinion of you? No worries about whether God is punitive, judgmental? No worries about His plan when your life as a human ends in this world? No worries about the possibility of hell or eternal damnation existing? Not worried about God being fed up with you for all the times you swore you'd pull your life around if only God would help you, and then repeated your errors again?

Not worried about whether God would listen to you or not? That God is fed up with you? That God considers you to be a hopeless case?

Now remember, if you make those kinds of judgments about yourself, you're going to believe that God will too. Why? Because what we think of ourselves, the human mind automatically thinks that others, including God, think the same way.

If God is ready to tackle such problem areas with you and enable you at this moment to see such issues, we have to address that first; nor is there anything wrong with you for having such concerns.

Proof that this is a common human problem is demonstrated by Jesus Himself. It is reported how Jesus had to pray three times in the Garden of Gesemane in order to prepare for being arrested. Three times Jesus asked His Father about whether He has to go through with His mission. Three times Jesus was reported to be aware of the uncertainty between His will and His Father's will. But we see no indication that Jesus was afraid of His Father's judgment of Him for having such a conflict!

Further proof is found in some of the last words reported to be said by Jesus while on the cross. A final human belief emerges from Him, in which He clearly states His belief that His Father has forsaken Him and asks His Father "why" this is so.

Is it coincidence then that Jesus reportedly said as His last words, "It is done" and thereby hands Himself over to His Father, Who then lifts Him from this world? Or did Jesus need that final reassuring answer in order to sufficiently feel safe to let go of any seeming value in this world and return to the true home? Had He discovered that indeed His human mind had deceived Him about His Father's actual love for Him? If the human mind can do that to Jesus, couldn't it certainly do the same with us?

Do you see that Jesus has shown us what we need to do if plagued by uncertainty of God's unconditional love of us? WHATEVER YOU ARE UNEASY ABOUT MUST BE GIVEN TO GOD FOR HIS DIRECT ANSWER! YOU CANNOT SETTLE THIS ISSUE BY YOUR OWN REASONING. WHY? BECAUSE YOUR HUMAN MIND IS CAUSING THE PROBLEM, AND YOU CANNOT USE THE MIND THAT'S CAUSING THE PROBLEM IN THE FIRST PLACE TO NOW PROVIDE A SOLUTION!

How do you give it to God? You'd straight out tell God about your distrust, and ask God to show you the matter the way God sees it, and wait for an answer. *"God, help me to see this as You do."*

But; suppose you say that you are even too frightened to do that? If that's the issue, then you've found still more of what you need to tell God. *"God I'm too frightened to even come to you, and could you help me to resolve my fear from Your viewpoint?"* You're permitting God to move upon you and bring you reassurance of His unconditional love for you. You're permitting God to show you how He looks upon you.

Why does God need your permission? Imagine a God Who ignores your desires and pace for turning to Him. Suddenly God acts upon you without your willing participation. You feel a force taking control of you, unbeknownst to you. You are caught in the grip of a change that you know not where it comes from or where it is leading. Do you recognize what that would do to you? God would have destabilized you. You would feel frantically fearful over this unwilling intrusion which takes away the control of your life.

Thus, God must work to gain your willingness to partner with you for healing and salvation, - NO MATTER HOW LONG THAT NEEDS TO TAKE. "Even months or years? Or lifetimes?" CORRECT! If God scares you by acting like a tyrant, even a seemingly benevolent one, it is a frightening and negative experience that would drive one further away from Him.

But eventually we all throw in the sponge. God has put in place some kind of supportive person or circumstance in front of us which supports our ability to turn to Him, ask His help with our fears and await His response.

And there is only one judgment God makes of us when we do or think in a negative manner; THAT WE'RE LOST, that we have no idea of our own divine nature or the divine nature of anyone else; and the lostness causes fear and negativity. Again, Jesus on the cross was teaching us about God's understanding of ourselves by calling upon His Father to forgive His tormentors because they have no idea whatsoever about what they're doing. *"Forgive them Father, for they know not what they do (Luke 23:34).*

You must have an answer to these issues. And until you become aware of God's answer, or as long as such problems plague you, you must continue to repeatedly hand them to God before you can go any further.

And; if you feel you're not getting an answer from God, what would you then pray? - "I don't hear an answer. Help me to understand why." Still no answer? Pray again and again until the Answer arrives and brings you the ability to act without fear.

No matter what thoughts you have about God, God wants them addressed to Him. Anger, sorrow, disappointment, fear, resentment; -they are the starting point for the beginning of relationship. And I can assure you from my own experience, that God knows how to respond back to you, and reassure you that peace and love between God and you is the only reality. Everything else is the twisted imaginings of the lost and fearful human mind.

Prayer

Before talking about my prayer style, let me mention the framework within which I talk to God. I have experienced God taking me out of the human dimension many times. I have seen in the spirit dimension that there is a healed me, free from hurt, concern and pain. I am at peace. I have no negative feelings or thoughts present. In the presence of God I feel open and welcoming of Him. The God that I experience would grant to me as part of my creation, the same joy, pleasure, contentment and fulfillment that He has. God would <u>never</u> hold anything back of Himself (except He can't make us the original Creator, which is His position alone).

Thus, when my soul returns to the awareness of heaven, all that gives God joy will give me joy. I'll settle for that any day!

So, then, what is there to pray for? Essentially, I pray when my human mind interferes and I'm unaware of the truth because my human mind is filling my head with nonsense. Anything that bothers me during that time, or another way of saying it,- when I forget that all is complete; -I'd be praying for some aspect of completeness to be "completed." I pray out of ignorance, -"*God let me see this as You do.*" Or, "*I want Your mind as my mind.*" Or, "*Be me, Love.*"

"Ignorance" is my forgetting that God has already taken care of the return trip to our home in heaven and our spirit identity. No slip ups. <u>Nobody is left out</u>. The divine Creation has continued to exist unchanged in its loving fulfillment from the cosmic moment when God enabled it.

I don't use a specific verbal formula for my prayers. Words can vary when I go in. Sometimes it's a simple *"Here"*, in which I offer myself to God. At other times it can be *"Take me over"*. Or, *"I choose Your Mind"*. Another form is, *"I choose You as Me rather than me as me."*

When I'm aware of the truth of completeness, I simply can be filled with "thank You(s)" and I'd offer myself to God for His usage of me to help where any sense of incompleteness exists either in me or others.

It's the same prayer for many different kinds of worldly circumstances, -sickness, natural disasters affecting others, all forms of troubled minds, etc. *"Love, help Yourself to me for whatever You wish to accomplish."* And then I let God make me as silent as God can get me to be. The silent me is the servant, used by God to heal my as yet unhealed issues, or through my mind to help others' minds seeking healing.

But when my human mind brings its belief in limitations to the existence of a loving completeness, then my prayers for myself or others can become very specific, and I'm praying for my "agenda" as I think God should act, rather than letting Him fulfill His agenda. I'll pray to make me well or somebody else well. That's my agenda. Do this God, as I think it should be done. Simply, I'm filling in for God's "incompleteness".

Another simple prayer is to use Jesus' words- *"Your will be done."* But what I want, no matter how I pray is to plain be humbled by God. I KNOW MY HUMAN MIND IS WORTHLESS AND I CHOOSE TO BE RID OF IT JUST AS SOON AS GOD CAN ACCOMPLISH THAT PROCESS. IN ITS PLACE I

NOW RECEIVE GOD'S MIND AS MINE AND TO ACT AT ANY MOMENT AS GOD WOULD. INCREMENT BY INCREMENT THIS GETS ACCOMPLISHED.

The other day, one of the members of our group asked if the human mind was absolutely worthless? That it could do nothing right? I told him that was correct. If we consider being "right" only how "God" answers, then every single attempt to answer our problems from our own head comes up short, and doesn't provide us with the ultimate God delivered answer. Doesn't that make sense to you, if you would have asked the same question?

Another issue I needed to understand through my prayer life was my attitude about receiving answers from God to my prayers. When I feel my completeness with God, it's never an issue. Not so when my head plays games with me. At that point I'm not seeing myself as a servant to God. Instead, I'm seeing God as a servant to me. Therefore, God should answer my prayers according to my own convenient standards I wish God to live by. Typical human mind twistedness. If God enables me to catch the issue, again I can pray- *"Thank you God, let me see this issue as You do."*

Does God love me? Of course He does! Does God want the healing process to proceed as quickly as possible? No doubt! God has stepped in once again to squelch the twistedness. God is in charge of the entire healing process, including the timing and sequence of addressing my healing progress and the processes by which it takes place.

Does my human head have an understanding of it? Never! Thus, I hand such uncertainties to God for

His resolution. God then enables me to remember He moves upon me as quickly as possible. After all, God is my loving parent, my loving Creator. Why would God want to do anything else but that?

Would God delay my healing or what service I can be in helping all God's children to return home to the kingdom? Of course not! Any thought of God being inattentive, or disinterested, or capable of brushing me off, is a product of my guilt ridden, negative, judgmental human mind and has nothing whatsoever to do with the reality of the complete, loving Being that God is.

But doesn't God have the capability to speed up the answers to you? Not without destabilizing you. Imagine feeling some force moving in you beyond your understanding, your participation in the process. You'd panic! Freak out! Think you were in some horror film!

GODMUSTWORKWITHINTHEBOUNDARIES OF WHAT YOU CAN SAFELY ABSORB. The human head has no awareness of and is incapable of making judgment about God's skillful workings within you. God must avoid your feeling frantic or out of control. It would drive you away from God in a state of fear if God so imposed upon you.

Maybe you'd also ask- *"Isn't my human head doing something right if I desire to pray?"* It's not your human mind that decided that. There is a portion of you that stands between your human mind and your God mind that is in charge of the direction you will turn to. Want more human "stuff"? You'll choose to feel the human. Want more "divine stuff" as your essence? Up comes you divine being into consciousness.

Have you ever heard the statement, *"Watch out what you pray for because you might get it?"* It insinuates that God would compel something upon you that would be unwelcome. It suggests that God would put you through something that you are not ready for. Human mind again. God only works within your potential and capacity. God is not going to disable and immobilize a precious servant helping to bring God's children back home. So, I don't fear God disabling me in the ministry that He wants me to accomplish. I don't worry about what I pray for.

Can I fail in my prayer life? Not a chance. My human mind can only DELAY ME from turning to God and addressing my Creator. God is aware of my mind's shenanigans, knows how many times it must prod me before I abandon them, and knows how to turn me away from the human temptations. God is in <u>perfect charge</u> of the timing and sequence of the healing process.

Suppose I pray some issue seeking a solution that is not in my interest? God would simply welcome the fact that I have sought communing with Him, but would never respond with a solution that is destructive to me. But God might as well use the moment to deliver healing on some other issue FOR WHICH I AM READY, never wasting the chance that I have given Him to be in contact with me.

Who is in charge of the expansion and maturing of my prayer life as I proceed in this lifetime? Not me. The human mind has no idea how to do that. It is God Who develops that within me. He's shown me only trustworthy qualities. I trust what God does with my prayer life and where it will lead me.

Despite everything that I've said so far about the perfection of God's leading me through the prayer practices, there are moments when all the above are ignored, and I press for an answer to a concern that needs solution according to my sense of its timing. Guess where it comes from? Of course. The human mind has intruded once again, trying to keep charge of the process in which I'm involved, and wanting God to be my servant rather than my being God's servant.

But eventually, God will enable me to place that issue before Him as well. "Lord help me to put my impatience before you and look upon the matter from Your eyes rather than mine." How often does it need to be done? As many times as our impatience rears up and until we've been returned to a comforting peaceful state of mind over the matter through God's initiative.

Meditation

I rejoice that God has enabled me to find Him. I rejoice that God began the process of talking with me some seven years ago and for the past five years it has been continuing on a daily basis.

I rejoice that God has been teaching me what healing encompasses and how salvation occurs.

I rejoice in His showing me that my human identity and the human mind behind it is not the real me.

I rejoice God has shown me there is another me, a spirit me, that will exist for all eternity and is of great worth to Him.

I rejoice that God has taught me how to deal with my human mind's attempts to down me, make me feel guilty, inadequate, lonely, weak and unlovable.

I rejoice that God has taught me of His willingness to live out my life in this world with me, and to provide me with His ways to handle circumstances and relationships exactly as He would.

I rejoice that my human mind distractions can no longer convince me that I am whom it says I am.

I rejoice that at any moment, when I desire peace and joy, worth and fulfillment, God delivers it to me.

I rejoice that God and I are inseparable in reality.

I rejoice that I am safe at last. Thank God almighty I'm safe at last.

I rejoice that you're safe at last. Thank God almighty you're safe at last.

I rejoice that God made meditation available to me by which all can realize and proclaim, "Hello heaven, goodbye world."

What's my job in meditation? What's God's job? My job is to simply want to reach for Him. Nothing more. And even that simple little wish has been nurtured by Him, because He increasingly shows me the treasures that result. That in turn, increases my yearning for still more of His presence.

I'd put the description of my job in another context. When all this started, I had no idea that I even was reaching for Him. So I'd say that my job was to recognize I couldn't go on any longer on the basis of what I knew about myself. I had hit my personal bottom, desperate for answers. I had gotten there.

What's God's job? God has now taken my life over, steadily and perfectly drawing me away from worldly values and replacing them with heavenly ones that will result in my return to my eternal home. I have been taught to become silent and wait for God to move upon me as many times during the day as God makes me aware to do so.

I might pause but for a moment. I might pause for thirty or more minutes. I might lose conscious awareness. I'm not in charge of the timing or frequency for the meditation process, nor its length of time. That is all determined by God and what God knows can be accomplished by me to fulfill His will and intention.

Nor am I in charge of the content delivered to me during a meditation. It might result in an experience of peace and quiet inside me. Or God's presence. Or a tingling feeling coursing through me. Or a warm sensation. Awareness of a need to forgive. A message informing me of remaining unhealed areas that require being further handed over to God. A compliment and encouragement that I'm doing well. Or, instructions about what He wants me to do for Him. Or, I feel contact with other people, either known or unknown. They are but a few examples of the infinite ways that God reaches out to us in His infinite wisdom by which to let us know of His presence with and in us. I simply wait for what God will deliver. God takes me into Himself inside of me. I let God take me there. I'm not active. I let God be the Activator.

Is there some specific way by which to practice meditation? Some people lie down, some sit. I'm a sitter. Some people look upwards with closed eyes. I look down and in. Some people have mantras, others visualize imagery. Some contemplate a scriptural passage. I'm silent. Some do it in company of others. Some do it alone. Some do it both ways. So do I. Some will hold hands with others to help with focus. Others find it a distraction. I do both ways with others depending on their preference.

If we get distractions, does this indicate we're doing something inappropriately? No. Virtually everyone mentions that they become distracted while trying to become quiet. There's good reason for being distracted. The human mind does everything it possibly can to pull us away from prayer and return us to human mind focus. And it will inevitably succeed in those attempts. It is normal. But God will make you aware of the distraction and enable you to return to the meditative stance. Didn't Jesus get distracted while praying in the Garden of Gesemane while preparing to go forward with His arrest? Didn't He have to return back into prayer three times? It will happen with us as well. The human mind distracts us, BUT CANNOT KEEP US.

Can we fail in a meditation attempt? No. If you even have the wish or desire to meditate, that is the beginning of the process, and as far as you can get at that moment, and should expect of yourself. That is success! Remember that God is in charge of what happens. God never exceeds your capability at any given moment. And just your simple yearn to be able to do it is a success. In time you will do more under God's continued guidance.

Some people will say after partaking in a meditation meeting that nothing happens. When you ask them if they tried to get in, invariably they will say they did try. But either they got distracted, or while trying, they believe that nothing happened. But when you closely question their experience as they initially entered in, they are helped to recognize that the "Nothing happened" which they reported was in actuality a quiet place, or a peaceful one, or an "empty" place.

When you ask them if their mind is usually empty, or quiet or peaceful, they can suddenly realize that they were, even for a few moments, apart from their noisy human mind. Thus, something did happen! Even constant distractions, either from thoughts of the human mind interfering or their listening to extraneous noises going on about them is the indication of the heightened effort of the human mind to pull them away from the activity. This happens because the person is indeed experiencing an inner presence which throws the human mind into high distraction gear. It too is the indication that they were on the right path!

What is accomplished by meditating? Two

things. First you will be experiencing the divine Presences in one way or another. That leaves an influence with you by which you become more and more like God. The divine Influence is taking you over.

The second aspect is that you become increasingly aware of the human habitation within your mind. The meditation process enables you to be aware of these unhealed areas and bring them to God's attention for His help in overcoming them. BOTH ASPECTS MUST BE PRESENT AS PART OF A FULLER HEALING. THE GREATER DIVINE EXPERIENCES BY THEMSELVES ARE NOT A FULL HEALING. A LIFETIME OF ATTENTION TO THE REMAINING HUMAN SHORTCOMINGS AND BARRIERS AND SURRENDERING THEM TO GOD ROUNDS OUT THE ELEMENTS REQUIRED FOR HEALING AND FOR THE SALVATION PROCESS TO DRAW DOWN TO ITS COMPLETION.

God Will Personally Contact You

Well, how did you do? Have these previous chapters encouraged you to try becoming silent, turning inward, and awaiting what God would intend to bring you?

If yes, then let's continue as we go into this chapter. But if not, let's pause for a moment.

One of the men in our substance abuse group mentioned "You know Bob, there's a part of me that's very comfortable with what you say, that I've got a divine mind and a human mind, and that being in the human mind causes all my difficulties. But I've got to be truthful, that although I'd like to reach for my divine mind, there's a part of me that's uneasy about doing it."

It turned out that he was uneasy about what that divine mind might be like. Because of the uncertainty, he was hesitant to move, because at least he knew what his human mind was like. I pointed out that it was a perfectly normal human reaction. After all, didn't the disciple "Doubting Thomas" state that he couldn't believe that Jesus had reappeared to them after He was crucified, and had to see it in order to believe it. And Jesus obliged him. Jesus knew what the human mind was like and what was needed to heal it. Jesus reappeared for Thomas's sake, and Thomas was enabled to safely believe.

Now the member had heard some testimonials from other group participants who had taken part in our silent prayer portions of our past meeting, and of the peace that they had felt. But it wasn't enough. We urged him, that when we went into prayer to mention to God his uneasiness, and ask God's help for dealing with it, because only God could give him reassurance to take a chance with what the product of his divine mind would be like.

Sure enough, he did it. He thought at first that "nothing happened." That's common with those of us beginning the process. Yes, he had gone in. Yes he had waited. And "nothing happened." We asked him to use other words to describe those moments of "nothing" happening. He used the words "quiet" and "restful". When we asked if his mind is usually that way, he could suddenly realize that this was not the usual state of his human mind! It dawned on him that he was indeed in another state of mind.

We asked him if he liked it. He readily agreed. I stated "That's the experience of your divine mind. "Nothing" happening is simply a mind that has no problems or issues bothering it. It's a mind that is one with God; and since God runs it as your mind, it knows all the answers in your life." It made sense to him. He smiled. At the end of the meeting he mentioned to me that he'd be back again next week.

So if you're interested, good reader, pause and see if you're ready to give over to God whatever is causing you the uncertainty. And if you have somebody who is a prayerful person, it can be helpful if you go into prayer together. It's reassuring (that's why Jesus sent His disciples out for their work in healing others two by two).

God does want you to feel safe and will respond to you. Just watch out for the tricks of the human mind that can claim "nothing" happened. You will be joyful when you experience God's contact with you.

Keep asking His help with whatever the thoughts are in your mind which have made you uncertain.

For those of us who have already gone in, you too might have been one of us who have thought that indeed "nothing happened" and I hope that the above was helpful to you. But again, try to find someone who uses silent prayer, or meditation, and share the experience with them. Or, you can always reach us at the Christian Laity Foundation through the various ways of communication that we make available.

Let's move on. What experience did you have? It is highly individual, for God is delivering every time exactly what you need at that moment to advance you in your understanding of your loving, divine identity, or God's loving presence, or your oneness with God, or your role in this world in helping others to find their healing and salvation path.

Before you went in, was your mind bothered with unsettling issues? Did you feel them lift? As though you now can handle them? That's what God would want- for you to handle them exactly as God would. That's what lifts burdens for our minds.

Or did you hear said to you "Everything is going to be all right." That's another one that a number of members experience. Sometimes it's not words but as a part of a feeling through which such assurance is given to them.

Some describe a feeling that a portion of themselves or maybe their whole self was suddenly being raised up, or was rising. At one meeting when we were holding hands with each other in the group, one member said that he felt one of his hands rising up accompanied by the hand that he was holding.

Then he felt it with his other hand and the one he was holding on the other side of him.

Some members experience what I refer to as "soul travel." They were gazing at family members, where they were and what they were doing.

Some see a bright light before their eyes, while their eyes are closed. Others see colors. Some suddenly feel very warm in portions of their body or the entirety. Some see angels, or God's presence. They are the ways God approaches each of His children with the most beneficial experience for which they are ready to receive at that moment. They are tailored for us by God for the continuity of our personal salvation pathway.

For myself, at different points of my own healing path, I've had any number of the above. And the "Footladder of Notes Divine" messages that God has delivered to me comes during the silent waiting.

What God will deliver each time is simply unpredictable. I encourage you to not even try to guess, or to try to plan what you would like to have happen. And make no judgment about what was accomplished! None! God is in charge of that! Our heads know nothing! Don't go in with the thought of a repeat of what has happened before. God is the better planner, knows far more what we need at any given moment of our lives and how to best deliver it. And if you are uncertain about it, ask God if that's so. When God responds to such issues, God settles them in your mind.

On occasion, a member will say that he or she felt fear when going into the silence. An unusual reaction, because God only brings peace and sense of safety and wellbeing when communicating with us. But when we go over the silence with the person we find that the fear was the last feeling that he or she felt and not the original feeling. The person reports that there was nothing of a negative nature when going in and only feels the fear when emerging from the experience. It becomes clear that the fear was the reaction of the human mind and not the experience of the meditative silence in itself. Indeed the human mind is uneasy about our reaching for God, as was pointed out before; and we can expect such reactions when we emerge from the meditative silence and become aware of the uneasiness in our human consciousness.

A final point. What's the payoff of the silence? You experience God's unconditional forgiveness of your own lostness and the lostness of others. You now begin to forgive as God's light in this world. You become the teacher of forgiveness to others. You are recovering awareness of your eternal soul and its oneness with its loving Creator. You are recovering the godly you that you were created to be in the first place.

You're learning to increasingly turn to God for direction of your life circumstances. You are being steadily groomed by God to continue the process of healing contact with our brothers and sisters for whom you have been given responsibility to help God with their path to salvation. You are into discipleship.

You increasingly know that the time when you have no peace means you're thinking again without God. Increasingly God helps you to become aware of those moments and rush back to the silent awaiting. Hello heaven, goodbye world. God's will is bringing me home!

At This Point of My Life

I'd like to report to you that each moment of the day I am in an angelic peace. Nothing bothers me. I have been enabled to devote each moment to meditation and prayer by which God can totally take me over. Not so.

Therefore, despite all the years I've devoted to achieving this, have I failed?

Absolutely not. My only job was to WISH TO GET THERE. It's God Who leads me into whatever I'm meant to accomplish. I'm still, though, in joy. Because I know that the peace of God is available to me from my Creator, and being perfectly delivered to me in incremental steps that I can safely absorb.

How about practicing absolute unconditional forgiveness for all hurts I experience from others? Intellectually I know this is what Jesus came into the world to teach.

The Spirit has gotten me far enough along that I know the reality and the precious worth of doing it. Forgiveness shines the light of God into the world. Is it the first spontaneous response that arises in me? It is not. My human mind continues to tell me that I'm vulnerable and threatened by other people's opinions or actions against me.

But God has gotten me to the point where I can recognize the nonsense of my unforgiving human mind. And even though I might not be able to stop an unforgiveness thought from being expressed, eventually God reaches me; and if I've acted negatively, God shows me how to make amends. God is on the job with me and will make me as forgiving as possible to fulfill His intentions through me during my remaining lifetime in this world.

Do I need others to love me to feel lovable? I do not. Only when my human mind has distracted me does this become a problem. But the human mind can't keep me. God has shown me that I have a choice. There is a loveable me, a divine me, made in the image of a loveable Creator. I'm complete within myself. The result of that completeness? Give it away to others. Teach how to get there. I need nothing in return, -no praise, no approval, nor acceptance. This "me" is a giver, with no need for taking.

Do I base my worthiness upon the judgments of others about me? I do not. The divine me is worthy and that is the true and only me in reality.

Is all this true of all God's children? Yes. We are made in loving oneness with each other and with God. My lost human mind can't see it. But when the divine mind is present to me, that truth emerges.

Is God always available to us to help us through our lost mind and the world it creates? All the time.

Are we all saved? Not so according to our human mind. But according to our divine mind, God brings every single one of His beloved creations to the process of awakening, to our divine nature and to its Kingdom home. Hello heaven, goodbye world. God's will is bringing me home!

Mental Illness

I've spent almost fifty years dealing with what the world calls "mental illness." The helping professions have huge diagnostic directories describing every form of troubled person, - depression, schizophrenia, psychopath, neurotic, etc. They speak of thinking disorders, emotional disorders and other descriptions of such people.

I'll have some fun with the groups I facilitate. I'll ask them if they want to hear my definition of what "mental illness" is. They know I'm mischievous, and they'll bite.

"Mental illness" I say, "is the result of the belief that there is no God, or a belief in a God Who can be unforgiving." That's a mighty broad definition, and includes a lot more people than the usual "professional" definition. But this to me is the core issue and a concern for all humanity. We've lost awareness of the qualities of our blessed eternal identity and its foundation in the unconditional loving nature of our Creator.

Frankly, if you're not aware of the loving God mind and presence as you, I say that's really being out of your mind! You've become a lost wanderer; indeed a desperate, frantic wanderer. OF COURSE, I'M SAYING THAT YOU'RE OUT OF YOUR GOD MIND.

And if the God mind and its processes are not available to you, you've deviated from how God made you in the first place. Jesus Himself said that in the human state He doesn't know anything and has to look to the Father for what He is supposed to do (John

5:19-20).

So what's my approach with those whom the world calls "mental patients"? I refuse to accept the world's definition. I will openly say to troubled people that I refuse to see them as "mental patients." I know who they are. They are God's beloved children playing that they are not. They are choosing to make believe that the human mind is real and their divine identity is not. I refuse to go along with the charade, and refuse to treat them as someone different than my own true identity. I give no credence to "nervous breakdowns" or chemical imbalances as core causality.

Of course I can play the game of being "out of my mind" also. Every single time that the human mind distracts me away from God, I'm "out of my mind" too. And until God enables me to catch on that it's happening, and provides me with the choice to let God get me back, I refer to myself as "wacky" or "nuts" too. I simply lost awareness of my spiritual self. Everything after that is an unreality, floundering in a human nothingness that is terrifying.

In fact, I rejoice that I can spot it, call it for what it is, and choose the return. Jesus even makes it easy for us to be gentle with ourselves. Look at His judgment about why people are out of their minds. He simply tells them that they don't know what they are doing (Luke 23:34). No knocking them. They'd stop what they are doing if they could know how to do so, but simply don't know how to stop.

So what the world calls "mental illness" is just a game we play of switching identities and then believing in the human one that we created as real!

The good news is that we can recover awareness

of our divine identities as God's beloved children. And we are shown that it was just a game we were playing that although very painful when we believed in ourselves as human, turns out to be nothing more than what a dream is similar to dreams when we sleep. Or a day dream, or fantasy when we indulge in them. It has no effect whatsoever on our true identity.

After all, God knows that if we come up with imagined identities other than the way He created us, -it has to be inferior! Thank heavens, God is the Chief Creator, and our imaginings can't change His creation of us! AND WHILE WE ARE IN THIS WORLD ALL OF THIS WILL BE SHOWN TO US IN ORDER TO HELP US RECOVER THE AWARENESS OF OURSELVES AS THE BELOVED CHILD OF GOD.

You might ask at this point, "O.K. then, how can we end the game of imagining a different identity than who we really are?"

I'll ask a question back- "Do you want to give up believing that you're a human body in the life of this world?" Do you want to throw away whom you think you are and await being shown whom you really are? How does it make you feel? Afraid of losing something? That's where a person with a so-called "mental illness" has to start as well, -just like us. Ready to throw away this world? Ready to call it worthless? Ready to let God take you to another world of what God says is of worth? Even if it's different than what your human mind claims is precious?

It's now seventy-four years for me. And there are many moments when I've not laid down my mind and said; "God, You're the only one Who knows what's right." I still can entertain the idea that I can come up with something right without God's presence. So I'm still having my "mental illness" moments too.

It must be that I'm still being suckered by my human mind into thinking that there is something of worth to hang on to, or I'm uneasy about the "product" of where God is going to take me too. I'm still investing faith in a mind another part of me knows to be absolutely worthless. Yet, there's a part of me that will even say it to God, -that "I'm a nothing in my human state. Flat out nothing! Take me over. Then I'm something in You!" Seventy-four years of working on this, back and forth. Obviously it's a careful process guided by God's awareness of how to balance my books.

Every single person who comes into this world must come to grips with this issue, not only those who the world defines as "mentally ill."

And the process brings with it the recognition of our lostness. Anxiety and depression precede the acknowledgment of our lostness, and of our hopelessness in finding a solution that is eternally fruitful. To even concede a small portion of lostness, maybe related to some moment in a situation or relationship, or a feeling about oneself, is sufficient for the process of healing to begin. We've recognized we're stuck. We've stopped!

For God needs that stoppage as a permission to come into our awareness inside of us. The joy of receiving God's solution for whatever issue constituted a "bottom", a moment in which we stopped, is now initiated. It now becomes a wedge into our human mind. It is a reminder that we found a precious satisfactory answer from the divine Source.

And that guarantees that we will be willing again and again to return to that Source. With that knowledge, there is now a lifting of our spirit out of the anxious and depressed state. There are solutions to every and all aspects of our lives!

Our healing is completely planned and in the hands of God. We are enabled to see increasing increments of worthless human mindedness and the depressive and anxious misery that it causes us. No longer are we at the mercy of the "mental illness" human mind. At last answers are known to us. God even directs us to supportive persons and groups to accompany us in the Holy Spirit led path. Oh the blessings of God's grace! Thank you God for the revelations. Thank you for Your love. Thank you for your loyalty. Thank you for our eternal souls. Thank you for eternal life and its God-like joys. Thank you for the prayer, "Take me over", or "Make me like You", or "Want You as me"! Amen.

Substance Abuse

Since Jesus reminds us that we're Gods (John 10:34), that life is in the spirit, and the body is nothing (John 6:63) then it strikes me that we in this world are all addicts, the addictive substance being the way of the world. People in this world are indeed largely consumed by its values and pleasures. They choose it over the life in heaven. We're addicts to it. That's why we stick around and want more.

When I'm with group members in our county jail who have worldly defined addiction problems (substance abuse), I inform them that I'm an "addict" too. My substance of choice is cookies. The only difference is that they are using what has been declared an illegal substance and mine is still legal. But if the powers of the world declare sugar cookies to be illegal, they should save me a bed in their jail dorm.

So, let's start this exchange between us with what makes me a "substance abuser".

First of all, substance abuse is not the cause of the essential problem. It's a <u>result</u> stemming from a troubling thought which people are trying to numb. That's the real issue!

Overwhelmingly others with whom I've held groups have told me that they drink or use drugs to cope with a feeling of unbearable loneliness. It's a form of self-medicating to turn off the feeling even though that anesthesia lasts for but a short while.

One particularly astute person said it was worse than "loneliness" for him; that the word didn't do the feeling justice. To him it was "isolation." I go with him- the ultimate loneliness evolves into isolation and that's what I experience when I head for cookie heaven.

The isolation comes from the feeling that you just can't share with another person how down deep degraded you feel. You'd be afraid to share it with someone else from the shame of what you feel about yourself. In my own human mind, I become immersed in feelings of insecurity. I feel needy. I want others to make me feel good. I'm a taker without any desire to give back. I feel neither self-esteem, nor worth nor any way to feel good. I feel like a guilty little kid wanting someone else to take care of me. That sure "isolates" you from daring to speak to someone about how you feel. You plain feel disgraced, immature and degraded.

If I'm in that human mindset for a second or longer, the very same feelings always arise. They never change. And the resultant impulse is to head for the cookie jar. I just want to fill up my empty feeling; kill it off with a dose of cookies. Make myself feel fed. And binge I will unless God gets to me and reminds me that my true "peace of God" mind is still available and awaiting my wish for God to shift me into it.

When I let God shift me, the neediness disappears. I feel lovable. I feel loving. I feel complete. I am again a giver. God is my completion. I need nothing else. Everything else simply fades away. The cookies remain untouched.

Tell me now- is what I described familiar to you too? Do I have your company in this self-description?

So, when I'm with our group members, I tell them they're not addicts. They are God's children who don't feel their true identity. And when we don't feel that identity, we lose awareness of our secure and reassuring Source of love. Losing that gives rise to the feeling of being unlovable. Now we're floating in a human mindset of a lost nothingness identity. We can't stand that feeling.

It's an absolute must to kill it off in some way. And drinking, drugs or cookies at least temporarily numbs the loneliness, self-degrading feeling.

How serious is that feeling? Members catch on quickly when I ask them what "rate" would increase as a problem if they had no way to numb it. They pipe up "The suicide rate!" I frankly tell them that until God can catch up with the loneliness issue, I'd never judge them for addiction substances they use in order to stay alive. It's better than killing themselves out of the desperation caused by believing there is no hope for their loneliness feelings, and it's too painful to stay alive. Even though incarcerated, the good news is that they're looking! That's why they're attending the group! And that's all God needs to reach them as quickly as possible!

So...can we make sense out of what addiction really represents? It's a desire to kill off the unbearable human feeling of deepest depression in a person who can't find any other way to head off the misery. Any way that person finds which temporarily wards off that awful isolation, and degraded judgment of oneself caused by not knowing to turn to God for His sustaining of us is to me some form of an addiction.

I share with others that the only answer I've ever found that works, which heads off my bee-line to the refrigerator is my prayer "Lord, Lord, Lord, (or Mother Mary or whomever you can pray too) I want

You as me" (or some variation of kissing goodbye to me as me), and to keep praying and praying it until the loneliness experience of the human mind dies down, and I recover that blessed inner peace of God's mind as mine.

And when the human mind comes back again? You have to expect it. The human mind is always hammering away. But when God enables you to be aware of it once again, you're ready for round two of prayer time, or round three, four, five, etc.

You might be asking, how does that praying ward off those down deep depressive feelings? Because when we ask for God's mind as ours, we get God's mind as ours; its rise into our conscious awareness. It displaces the human mind at that point simply because you wanted It to displace it. In the God mind as yours, there is no neediness. God is complete. Thereby; since that is the reality of the God-like you, you're complete. No needs. No down feelings. No depression. You become the "giveaway" portion of God, passing on to others that there is another alternative for the same suffering in their life that has been in yours. There's no need to "take." The complete joy that you feel in that state comes from your yearning to give it away to others. That's the God mind as you. It's yours for the asking!

If Jesus sent out His disciples two by two, might you suspect that we too need a "support" figure or group? Six out of seven days in the week I'm engaged with my support network!

Oh yes, I'll take it. Hello heaven, goodbye world. God's will is bringing me home!

Criminality

We've spoken about what the world calls the mentally ill. We've spoken about what the world calls substance abusers or addicts. Now we move on to the people who commit what the world calls criminal acts.

Let me ask you a question. When you hear of some horror story, spousal abuse, killing of adults or children, child abuse, robbery, rape, etc., is your first reaction to such happenings one of fury against the perpetrator(s)? Do you get around after that first reaction to considering whether this is another aspect of peoples' lost identities and crushing fears being the driving force behind such behaviors? Yes? No?

Do you want to entertain understanding of why this happens, or simply look at the perpetrators as pure evil, and simply view punishment as the main approach?

I've spent some twenty years of my professional life dealing with criminal behavior amongst those declared mentally ill by the justice system. My frank and open answer about criminal behavior is that the same human mind issues relating to substance abuse and mental illness relates to those we call "criminals." I'll go one step further. Prisons are a product of the blind human mind. We deny that the same impulses are in ourselves. They "purposely do their criminal acts", so says our human minds, and punishment is the only answer.

I offer my own view to you about criminal behavior. The essential questions become- do they experience themselves and others as being divine? Do they feel God's love for them and all others? Obviously not. If you experience yourself as holy and lovable, then you know the other person is the same as you. You would neither do something harmful to yourself nor to another. Also, you never feel threatened by negative self-opinions, nor negative opinions about you from others. They bounce off you as meaningless, and you have no need to defend yourself against them.

Your attitude while you are in that sacred world is simply to give away the love that you feel in order to help others feel the ultimate joy of their divine nature. Nothing else matters or gets priority over this- the helping of others to be healed and return to the kingdom. What bolsters this attitude is the knowledge that God is within you, leading you in this world, taking good care of you until your job is done, and then returning you to eternal life and its joys.

Your experiences have also assured you that God is very reliable in these matters. No needs. No worries. No survival issues. You're just a well-taken-care-of servant doing a divinely guided job in this world.

So, can we accept that those who do criminal acts are quite unaware of all this? Can you accept that they have the same human mind as ourselves with the same aggravations with which they have to contend? Can we accept that they feel just as insecure as ourselves? If yes, let's go on. If not, the rest of this is difficult for you to absorb. It would be meaningless, just not your experience of these matters at this time.

When we're down on ourselves, the first reaction is to be depressed. We don't know why we're down on ourselves, but maybe if we beat ourselves up enough as a penance, if we feel crushed enough, maybe, we'd feel better. That's classic depression. We've no idea that the human state has built into it a guilt feeling that comes from our experimenting with being different from the way God made us as eternal spirits. That causes guilt, depression and fear of God. That's a whopper of a fear. It's our guilt feelings that cause our fears of God. And sadly we don't ask God how to look at this issue as He does.

Criminals, like us, have the same issues. Whereas we might get depressed and turn on ourselves, criminal behavior against others takes another step to deal with the crushed human psyche. They will believe that others feel about them the way they feel about themselves. They don't realize that it's their own beliefs about themselves that they are attributing to others. It's "others" who don't give a hoot about them.

Everybody becomes the enemy. They feel very threatened. There are no loopholes by which to get out of this reasoning. And savagery becomes a justifiable behavior for survival.

Maybe you can see this from another viewpoint. The attack upon others is the criminal's way of saying "You don't care about me. You don't love me." So, the attack is really a raging call from someone who feels unlovable, to others to make him feel lovable. It's a rather inefficient way to accomplish it, but that's all the criminal has got going for themself at that point.

Really, it's just like the depressed person hoping that if enough penance gets performed and they become crushed enough, maybe someone would love them.

So the criminal feels nobody gives a hoot for them, and the only way to survive is to "take" what nobody else would want to give them, be it love, food, material things for survival, etc. It's the only way to "get." It's now justifiable to hurt others, e.g.: rape, assault, kill.

Punishment as others' response to them only convinces them that they're right, and delays further their opening to the healing that God's waiting to deliver to them.

Can you recognize criminality to be one more extension of the lost human mind? Can you recognize that the answer to it is for the person to be in a secure facility that prevents further acting out against society while providing the spiritual healing support that offers hope? -that there's a spiritual solution for which he's just as eligible as the rest of us lost humans? We need at this point to ask, "Did we have a support system by which we turned away from the lostness of our human mind? Are criminals a demonstration of how lost and savage the untamed human mind can become? Are they a hint to us of 'But for God I'd be there too?"

Hope this little tidbit was helpful, good hearts. They're my brothers and sisters just like anyone else feeling a "franticness", recognized or unrecognized, that I can identify with. And, I feel I can understand what has led them to act the way they do, even the most horrendous crimes. Or criminally turning on themselves and committing suicide. It's just the pits of lonesome terror inside of all us humans if we feel there's no hope. It kills us...and results in killing others as well. And God knows how to heal us all when we get to the point of reaching for it. Spiritually supportive circumstances and relationships get us there more quickly.

Forgiveness

Can you see that we're working our way towards the single issue that is behind all healing and final salvation? It's forgiveness of ourselves and others.

If we say that to be healed and saved we have to recover the Christ mind as our mind, that this is the ultimate goal,- the "kingdom" within us- then to the extent we are accomplishing the recovery of that divine state within us, we are progressing on the path to healing and salvation. Where Jesus is, we're getting there too.

Here's another way by which to look at its importance for us. Jesus has pointed out that we've got to depend on God to deliver the elements of healing and salvation. But, if we're down on or unforgiving about ourselves, how in heaven's name can we go to God with any feeling of safety, if we feel God could be down on us too? Now that's scary. Remember now that what we feel about ourselves is exactly what we believe that others, including God, feel about us too! It's called projection.

You might say to me that there are people who go to God; and they are not completely forgiving, particularly of others. Or maybe they still can't forgive themselves yet as fully as they feel is required. Such folks don't know why they keep asking God to forgive them as though that was the issue, when in actuality the problem is they can't fully forgive themselves or others. Their progress is frozen at that point until God finds the way to enable them to open more fully. They remain vulnerable to the human mind's limited "forgiveness" (I'll forgive you, but I won't forget) and their mind's fear of God viewing forgiveness just like they do.

What we're all working our way towards is the prayer to see, understand and thereby forgive as God would. What are the required elements for that type of prayer? What must we know before we can "risk" such a prayer?

We must be shown that we are divine beings, immune to being destroyed in any way. We must have the experiences of that truth. Just believing it is not enough. We must <u>know</u> it as our personal experience.

Once we become aware of our invulnerability, we know that nothing of what others do to us, and nothing of what we do to ourselves can hurt the eternal spirit being that we truly are. We know that the human "self" is but a mask we put on. There is the greater "me" that sits behind it. It's another self, another world, another reality, separate and apart from this fantasy world that we've cooked up as our playground...a very unhappy playground indeed.

Once we experience that self, we are driven by entirely different motivations than what drives the human mindset.

We experience God within us and God's drive to help His children to recover awareness of their eternal divinity through us, His servants. This is the loving thought, the singular loving thought that now drives us. Nothing else is of value except to bring that to others.

That's the ground upon which Christ's forgiveness was established. The God mind in full bloom is now increasingly our mind. We know that behind the mask of difference and separation from each other, we are still one with each other. We are a loving completeness in that eternal oneness with each other. And we know that oneness to be the oneness that God feels with us as well.

If you ask me whether I've experienced that, the answer is yes, except when my human mind intercepts my awareness. And the catching of that distraction is the signal that another increment of forgiveness is ready for delivery to me by God for the portions of my mind awaiting further healing.

I know that beyond my awareness the process is complete in me. Always was, always will be. And God is delivering the awareness of that completeness very gently, just as fast as I'm enabled to see it and practice it with myself or with others. And of course, what unforgiveness still exists about others indicates you believe the same is unforgivable in yourself.

What do you think? Should I forgive myself for not as yet being open to the full practice of the kingdom's complete forgiveness? Or chew myself out for not having advanced further at this time?

I'll choose to forgive myself, for God is my Deliverer. My only job was already accomplished. I told God to "go ahead and move on me." Job completed on my part. The rest is God's. Do you agree in this for yourself? Do you feel ready to go to God and ask to see forgiveness for yourself or others only as God does? It's the path to recovering our heavenly home. See you there soon. Hello heaven, goodbye world. God's will is bringing me home!

Guilt

I had disappointed my mother. Her ninety-second birthday was coming up, and I made travel plans to visit her. But before the day of traveling I was not feeling well, called the travel agency to re-book my flight, called my mother and informed her of it. I heard the sadness in her voice.

Mom passed away before I could get there. Her caregiver had felt she was not in a crisis, told me to call her the next day before running down on an emergency flight. Mom passed away that next day.

It's seven years later, and even in writing this now, I once again feel badly that I could not have gotten there; guilt, remorse, self-reproach over having done what I felt was wrong. I feel that I should have had the strength to go through with it. I had backed away instead of trying to go, no matter what was wrong. Does it touch a chord with you? In some personal circumstance of your own?

Have you done something that guilt can still get to you? A weak moment? Or hurt someone? Or even a crime that still disappoints yourself or others in their attitude towards you?

Why is it important to look at this issue? Because if we get down on ourselves, we believe that God too can be down on us, disappointed in us, disapproving of us, even punitive towards us. And since these writings are about letting go of this world and recovering the awareness of the heavenly one, we delay our return by being worried about the judgment of God. AND WE NEED TO TRUST GOD IN ORDER TO BE WILLING TO RETURN TO HIM.

Guilt is fine as a starting point, the sign we are aware of wrong or hurtful thoughts and actions. Repeated or continuing feelings of guilt are acceptable only in that they compel the need to seek a solution to the matter, or to be healed of what has happened, or to gain a perspective over past occurrences and be able to overcome these issues if they should arise in the future. ONLY THEN ARE GUILT FEELINGS ACCEPTABLE.

But guilt has no worth after that, nor does remorse nor self-reproaching. It's a meaningless approach that brings no relevant resolution.

Let's take apart the issue I laid out with my mom's passing. What's your opinion? Shouldn't I have had the inner strength to go through with the trip no matter how I was feeling? My human mind used that in its playing with me, to depress me. My answer to "I should have," or "I could have" is "NOT SO!"

At any moment in our lives we are either capable of acting or we are not capable of it. There's no way around it. Either God gives you the strength that allows you to act, or you cannot. With me, the strength and insight was not yet available to me to deal with feelings of sickness. I had even prayed my feelings state a number of times and still could not act upon it.

Jesus prayed too in the Garden of Gesemane for the strength to permit Him to go through with His arrest. He prayed once. He did not receive it. He prayed twice. He did not receive it. In great stress, He prayed a third time before finally feeling the inner strength from His Father to enable Him to move forward.

In retrospect, would I have liked to pick up the strength to go through with the trip? Of course. But it's meaningless. It simply was not available to me at the time. God had not gotten me to the point where I could feel His strength as mine. That was what I would have needed to overcome my human mind and its depressive nature.

I mentioned, as well, that even as I write this, my head played its usual game; and I winced in sadness at the memory. Based on what you've read so far in these chapters, what would you suggest to me that I do when my head comes at me with its downing influence?

Let's look at some prayer options:

"God, forgive me for my past weaknesses."

"God, forgive me for my sins."

"God, take away these feelings."

In the first two prayers, I'd be thinking that God hasn't forgiven me, is down on me, and I want Him to change His outlook towards me. Any number of people whom I have known never get relief by praying these prayer examples despite the hundreds of times they have repeatedly prayed that. It's of no help to me to do so either.

The third prayer I feel to be a bit more relevant. I'm recognizing the problem is mine. It's my thoughts that are bothering me. But now I'm instructing God how I WANT the feelings handled; "Take the feelings away." Maybe that's not the solution according to God's understanding of what I need. So, it's presumptuous. I'm not trusting God to handle the issue on His terms. I'm setting the way I want God to act.

How we doing? Do you agree? Disagree? Whichever way you feel is fine. I won't oppose you. It's just that those prayers don't do anything for me.

I pray now as I type this:

"God let me see this matter as you would want me to." That's pretty much the same prayer as Jesus in the Garden saying, "Not my will, but your will be done." Indeed, as Jesus received His peace within Him from His Father, I too notice the quieting inside myself. My discomfort has abated and the issue is no longer there. I'm at peace.

Jesus explained why that peace will come. He stated, "Father, forgive them for they know not what they do (Luke 23:34)." That brings me peace. I have been taught by God that when my troubled human mind kicks in and can for the moment distract me, with its guilt, negativism and judgmentalism, I can choose God's compassionate perspective and get it. Every moment is simply a choice between my human mind or my divine mind, the latter being one with God in me.

WE SIMPLY NEVER KNOW WHAT WE ARE DOING. AND EVEN IF WE SAY THAT WE KNEW IT WAS WRONG AND DID IT ANYWAY, I SAY TO THAT- NOT SO! BECAUSE, WE DID NOT YET HAVE THE POWER TO ACT ON IT! WE MUST WAIT FOR GOD TO DELIVER STRENGTH TO ACT! THEREFORE, "WE KNOW NOT WHAT WE DO!"

I hope this little story's perspective helps bring you the peace of God that reduces the amount of delay in declaring, "Hello heaven, goodbye world." Let God show you His perspective about your guilt, and how to look upon yourself. God's understanding and solutions are helpful and meaningful. The ones that come from our human minds? Worthless!

The Needless Fear of Death

I've mentioned to you that I know "death" does not exist. God has shown me that I am not a body. I am a spirit being. I've seen the spirit me. I love it. I want it. It's always at peace, feels loved and has a sense of belonging with God and everyone else.

I also know from that identity that God gives all of us a joyous eternal life. What gives pleasure to God would be given to us. There is no doubt about it in my mind. NONE WHATSOEVER... when I remember the state of consciousness of my divine identity.

So, good hearts, explain this one. I wound up in the hospital a few months ago after having heart palpitations, sudden surges of my heart speeding up, breaking out into a sweat and increasing exhaustion in each of those episodes.

Usually there is one episode, after I've eaten something that produces stomach gas, which passes over after a while. The reason for the episodes stems from the fact that I have a hiatal hernia. A physician explained to me that when gas forms in my stomach, it can push through the hernia into the cavity where the heart is located and cause interference with its usual and proper functioning. My heart then becomes erratic.

But, this was going on for an extended period of time. I had an upset stomach in the first place; but tried to continue to eat in my usual fashion at home. As a vegetarian, I eat certain foods that do produce gas but for which I take a "gas pill" that controls any excessive production; so, it doesn't bother me. But not this time. Despite my taking the pills, I would now have repeated attacks of heart disturbances. And they were exhausting me. I made the decision to go to the hospital. I could not understand why they would not stop as they had done in the past. I was frightened.

To my delight, the hospital had vegetarian meals, with some really great tasting veggie burgers that I kept downing. And shortly after each meal more heart episodes would begin. And they took a greater toll on my energy levels from their repeated occurrence. I finally reached the point where I decided I was in the midst of heart failure; that my heart was steadily weakening from continued attacks, and that I was dying. I WAS FRIGHTENED!

I didn't believe that I was going to make it to the next morning at the rate this was going on and informed the nurse. She replied that I was on some kind of monitoring device and that nothing was showing which supported my experience. (In retrospect I wonder what it was monitoring.) But her reassurance did not change my fear thought that these were my last hours on earth.

In my fright, I now turned to God and spoke to Him (and Mary too), reviewed the reassurances that I had known from the past contact with Them that would give me peace, and said it was Their business and not mine when I'd leave this world, that my life was theirs and finally got to sleep, wondering if I'd leave town around four A.M., which I had read somewhere seemed to be the time when many souls departed. I awoke about 6 A.M.; and I was still alive!

In came the physician a few hours later who confirmed what the nurse had said, but made a suggestion to me. "Dr. Weltman, I know you are a vegetarian, but for the time being would you mind ordering a cheese sandwich instead of those veggie burgers which are very gas producing?" I did, and within another day I was discharged from the hospital.

What started all this? The combination of a stomach upset plus an unrelenting diet of my veggie burgers repeatedly was stressing my heart.

But let's get to the other issue. How come I was so distressed about dying? Have no doubt about it. I was frightened about the prospect of dying, that I was on the way out.

Let me turn the table though, for a moment. Put yourself in my position, in which you believe that you're going to die within a very short period. Just pause now. Are you ready to go? Is there an inkling of fear? A cold discomfort? An uneasiness? You're going to leave everyone and everything that you know. You don't know what's next in the fullest sense. Now, are you afraid of death, or at the moment you think about it, do you feel an uncertainty about your personal worth, an immaturity, a shame, guilty feelings, a concern about whether you'll "belong", or be wanted? Or even worse, do you have fears of punishment, rejection, maybe hell as real?

Back to me. My fears arose from the breaking in of my human mind, and its characteristic downing of me. Even then I knew there was no death as such. I knew I was eternal. But when the possibility hit of my moving on, I was fearful about the qualities of myself as I experienced myself in my human mind. Immature, a taker, wanting others to take care of me, do for me, etc… It was this human me that I was afraid of. It won't be welcome. It won't belong.

When I'm in my divine mind, these characteristics are not experienced. But when I am seduced by the human mind, my fears of not belonging rise up. The fear of death is not the fear of death. It is my fear of not belonging. Loneliness. Isolation. "Does anybody want me?"

So, to summarize, is there death? No. We never die. We exist forever, or to put it another way, as long as God exists. The human mind causes, in the first place, a fear of death itself until we find out that we shed our bodies; but they are not the real, the ultimate "us". Our divine self goes on. All that can bother us even after we know we are eternal, is the machinations of the resurfacing human mind which makes us fear our own qualities as a human being. Did you spot that when you tried out looking at your own leaving of this world? Hope you did. Hope you saw that it has nothing to do with death, but with our down feelings about our human self. It's quite a relief to know that. When I got there I was able to get ready for God bringing me home, if I was leaving at 4 A.M. Hello heaven, goodbye world. God's will is bringing me home!

Hearing God's Voice

All of us will experience the presence of God. One of the ways that is my experience is to focus on messages or thoughts that unfold in my mind. They occur when I offer myself to God for His service, and wait within me for however God will reveal His presence. I can remember one time when I actually heard a Voice. It occurred during a meditative silence. He called me, "Bob." It was soft, quite gentle; but more than anything else, God said it to me in such a way that I knew I was loved.

So maybe using the word "Voice" restricts too much our understanding of the ways by which God reaches out to us. A touch on the cheek, a feeling of a warm energy within our body, or even a cold chill, or a sense of a worry or weight being lifted from us, or an out-of-body experience, or a sense that all will be o.k.- the ways are countless. As many of His children there are, - that receipt of His presence is highly individual, and none of the ways is better than some other way. God knows the best way to make His presence known to each of us and the "message" that it conveys.

A dear friend asked? But how do we know it is God?" Have you had an experience yourself which has left you with that question? There's a very simple rule that I go by. If it brings me a sense of peace and reassurance, it's God's presence. But you might say that you felt fear in the moment, not peace.

If you felt fear, you can be sure that's not from God. But when you look carefully at your experience, think about when the fear surfaced. People will consistently report that it was <u>after</u> the divine experience, WHILE EMERGING FROM IT. This is invariably our human mind's reaction to the presence of God. But when we inquire further, we find there was a different emotional feeling before the fear emerged. It's reported as a peace, of quiet, or a reassurance, or a serenity, etc... Then they realize that indeed God had originally been present to them.

Now, if you're still puzzled or uncertain about your personal experience, let me make one more suggestion, which would be what I would do if it was needed. Just ask God. "Beloved, help me to look upon my uncertainty about Your presence within me as You know it to be." You're asking for God's interpretation instead of your own human thinking.

You'll know then whether your experience was legitimate. Because God knows the way to deliver that to you in such a personal way that it removes all doubt.

You might ask, "How come God didn't settle it for me in the first place and I need to go back to Him?" It's reported in Scripture that Jesus stayed out all night praying before He picked His disciples the next day. Didn't Jesus also have to pray three times in the Garden of Gesemane before being able to let Himself be arrested? What caused it with Jesus and what causes it with ourselves?

It's the human mind "horning in" to move us away from God. Does God know He has to deal with our doubts as one more of the human mind's tricks? Of course.

It's God's job to know how to deal with the human doubts and uncertainties that most assuredly are going to plague us on the path of our healing. And suppose after asking God about the validity of your experience, you're still uncertain. What then? God will patiently teach you to ask again and again until He can get the message through to you. It's needed. Absolutely normal. It's not a sign of failure.

In Conclusion

Is there one prayer more than any other that I seem to lean on for getting me through my life in this world and the return to heaven? Is there one that I find to be the most encompassing? Is there a prayer that seems to fit many situations, personal relationships, fears, uncertainties, etc...? I think so.

"Love, take over. I want You as me" seems to be used quite frequently by me. I've got different ways of saying it so that it's not always the same words. It can be "Here Love, run my show." Or "Only You, Love, only You." Or "Move it Love, quick." Or "Want You, not me." Or, "Possess me."

Why does it work? I've abandoned my human mind where all the fears and guilt and inadequacies reside. I'm not focused on them anymore. They can't control that moment. I'm not invested in that mind. I know it's a liar. It has no truth whatsoever.

What do I get in its place? First; the disappearance of whatever is bothering me. It simply dies down. And where there was negativity and fear, now there is a peace. A sense of confidence. A reality that I have now allowed God to take over, and it's no longer my business to handle the moment with my flawed mind. It's now God's business to handle my affairs. And it is God Who is responsible for whatever is meant to be accomplished. I'm free of judgment of myself, criticism, self-definition of what is success and failure, or competence and incompetence. No more shame or disgrace or embarrassment over my standards of what should be accomplished. It's all God's business.

Will it last? Nope. My head wangles its way

in again and its back to conflict and fear. But I don't worry about it. God comes once again, reminds me of where I am, and I simply pray it again. Just like Jesus in the garden trying to get ready for the completion of His ministry. I know that no matter what I'm going through, in the long run God wins out; and I'm in very safe hands.

Two issues constantly repeat themselves with me; surrender of myself to God and forgiveness of others. Both can be barriers to where God has to get me in order to be a servant to Him in this world, and then be willing to return to the spirit world of heaven. Surrender requires that I see no value in my human mind and existence. Surrender requires that I see the human state brings me constant conflict and chronic uneasiness for which I have no solution. And the prayers that I have mentioned above are applicable to this issue. "None of me Love, all of You." Day after day our human minds resist this turn to the spiritual. But we cannot be stopped. Delayed- yes. Stopped- no.

Without surrender, the forgiveness issue cannot be resolved. The human mind will not see the lost state in ourselves or others. Returning to heaven involves the awareness of our true oneness of our souls with each other, and this too must be accomplished through prayer life. But once the surrender issue is being addressed, the forgiveness issue takes center stage.

The surrender has permitted God to show me I am an eternal being. The events of this world are simply a stage play totally irrelevant to the spirit world. My soul in its purity remains untouched. The human mind has no influence on the soul's permanent loving nature. It's all a game. A painful one indeed, when, we believe in the reality of it and have no awareness of our spirit self. But, no more than a game.

Now we are no longer invested in the safety of the human identity and of our body. Thus; we can turn to God and ask to see the other person as God does- someone as lost as us and having no idea of how to re-emerge from it. It is now safe to forgive. And we do so, because our divine mind finds that natural. Anything else would be preposterous. Our loving spirit nature now is in charge. Our Godliness leads us. The practice of forgiveness is the essence of ourselves as disciples, healers, agents of salvation. Servants of the Most High becomes our one identity in this world teaching the practices of surrender and forgiveness.

You and I take our turns at being healed and being healers of others. The process is perfect. God never gave us any choice about changing ourselves from how He created us. The timing of when our healing starts is ours;- all the rest is a foregone conclusion directed by the God Who is determined to bring all of His children home. God's plan is complete. Seen it. Want it. The show is over. We wait our turn to be called, with increasing confidence in God's delivery of healing grace and love. All works out in the end. See you there! Hello heaven, goodbye world. God's will is bringing me home!

About the Author

Dr. Robert Weltman, a clinical psychologist, received his PhD from Yeshiva University in 1964. After years of employment with a New York State Department of Mental Health psychiatric center, private practice, and becoming Director of Counseling for a college, Dr. Weltman went on to become the head of Psychology of a New York State forensic psychiatric center for the dangerously mentally ill and criminally insane from which he retired in 1994.

As part of his professional career he also helped children and adults with neurological and developmental problems by creating techniques for treatment and diagnosis coordinated with a neurosurgeon and optometrist. This methodology maximizes the potential for patient progress by capitalizing on the joint knowledge of the different professions. This experience helped him to recognize the value of utilizing multiple methodologies in helping mentally challenged people reach their full potential and promote healing.

As part of his personal searching for more effective treatment methods for the troubled mind, Dr. Weltman turned to the role of spirituality in healing. Through deep meditation and prayer, Dr. Weltman experienced the Judeo-Christian presence of the God of love. Coupled with this, Dr. Weltman now became aware of his own true spiritual nature and that of all people.

Even though he was raised and educated in the Jewish tradition, Dr. Weltman's personal journey in the spirit dimension led him to be additionally baptized as a Christian in 1986, fusing it with his Judaism. Twelve years later, as part of his daily meditations, he would then receive from God the healing curriculum entitled, *"Footladder of Notes Divine"*. The daily dictations began in 1998 and continue to the present day.

Dr. Weltman's life experiences have shown him that the path to personal healing is through the God-led realization and recovery of the spirit nature we all share and our eternal soul's ultimate goal of returning home to its Creator. Because of this, Dr. Weltman was divinely instructed to establish the Christian Laity Foundation, a not for profit organization that teaches and supports a skilled prayer and meditative life conducive to healing and salvation. In turn, the Christian Laity Foundation established "Spiritual Healing Radio", an on-air broadcast dealing with our human issues and problems, and a You Tube Channel entitled, "Healing Aspirations" devoted to topics that inspire healing, well-being and peace of mind.

If you're interested in learning more about Dr. Weltman and his healing curriculum, please visit his website at **www.christianlaityfoundation.org**. Here you can order his books, listen to archived broadcasts and YouTube® shows and gain access to long awaited revelations regarding Mary – The Mother of Jesus and persons with Down's Syndrome and Autism.

Notes

Notes